Living the Karma Way: A Practical Guide to a Fulfilling and Harmonious Life

Randy Woodrum

Published by Randy Woodrum, 2024.

LIVING THE KARMA WAY: A PRACTICAL GUIDE TO A FULFILLING AND HARMONIOUS LIFE

First edition. January 19, 2024.

Copyright © 2024 Randy Woodrum.

ISBN: 979-8224378135

Written by Randy Woodrum.

Table of Contents

Living the Karma Way

A Practical Guide to a Fulfilling and Harmonious Life

In the tapestry of existence, the threads of our actions weave a complex pattern, shaping the canvas of our lives. This intricate interplay is the essence of karma—an ancient concept that transcends cultural boundaries, offering profound insights into the nature of our deeds and their far-reaching consequences. "Living the Karma Way" is an exploration of the timeless wisdom embedded in the philosophy of karma and a roadmap for cultivating a life of purpose, mindfulness, and positive influence.

In the hustle and bustle of modern living, the pursuit of happiness often leads us down diverse paths, each laden with its own set of challenges and choices. Yet, at the core of our journey lies the undeniable truth that our actions reverberate, creating an intricate tapestry that reflects the energy we contribute to the world. Drawing inspiration from Eastern philosophies, this guide invites you to embark on a transformative journey—a journey that transcends the superficial and taps into the profound wellspring of karmic understanding.

Our exploration begins by unraveling the threads of karma, dissecting its three distinct forms: the accumulated actions of the past, the current actions shaping our present, and the seeds we sow for the future. Through this understanding, we gain insight into the interconnected nature of our choices—a web of cause and effect that binds us all. From this foundation, we will explore practical techniques for cultivating mindful awareness, setting positive intentions, and fostering compassion—essential tools for navigating the intricate dance of karma.

"Living the Karma Way" is not a mere philosophical treatise; it is a hands-on guide, offering tangible practices to integrate karma into your daily life. From the power of intention to the transformative potential of responsibility, each chapter provides actionable steps, empowering you to shape your destiny consciously. We explore the profound impact of empathy, the importance of detoxifying the mind and body, and the role of positive relationships in creating a harmonious existence.

As we navigate this journey together, remember that living the karma way is not about perfection but progress, not about judgment but understanding. It is an invitation to embrace responsibility, practice self-compassion, and build a life that resonates positively with the world around you. In the pages that follow, discover the transformative power of mindful living—a journey toward a more fulfilling and harmonious existence.

Karma, derived from ancient Sanskrit, encapsulates a profound understanding of the interconnected nature of human actions and their consequences. Rooted in Eastern philosophies, karma is not merely a cosmic ledger of rewards and punishments but a dynamic force, an intricate web weaving the fabric of our existence. At its essence, karma is the universal law of cause and effect, positing that every intention and action sets forth a series of reactions that inevitably shape one's destiny. It emphasizes the idea that our present circumstances are influenced by the sum total of our past deeds, urging individuals to be mindful of their choices and cultivate a consciousness that extends beyond the immediate moment. Beyond a fatalistic concept, karma serves as a guiding principle for ethical living, emphasizing responsibility, compassion, and the realization that our actions reverberate far beyond our immediate awareness.

The historical and cultural context of karma is deeply rooted in the spiritual tapestry of ancient Indian philosophy, particularly within the realms of Hinduism, Buddhism, and Jainism. Originating from the Sanskrit word meaning "action" or "deed," karma transcended the boundaries of religious doctrines to become a foundational concept in the spiritual fabric of various Eastern traditions.

In Hinduism, karma is intricately woven into the cycle of reincarnation, where one's actions in a past life shape their current existence and influence future rebirths. Buddhism, emerging as an offshoot of Hinduism, adopted karma with a nuanced perspective, emphasizing the potential for liberation from the cycle of birth and death through mindful actions and enlightenment. Jainism, too, integrates karma as a fundamental force, shaping the soul's journey through a cycle of birth and rebirth.

The cultural resonance of karma extends beyond religious contexts, permeating daily life in many Eastern societies, shaping ethical frameworks, and influencing societal norms with an emphasis on personal responsibility and the interconnectedness of all beings.

In Eastern philosophies, the concept of karma transcends a simplistic cause-and-effect relationship, offering a profound understanding of the interconnected nature of existence. Rooted in spiritual traditions, karma is a dynamic force shaping the destiny of individuals and communities alike. It searches into the intricate web of actions, intentions, and consequences, suggesting that every thought and deed contributes to a cosmic balance. Collectively, Eastern philosophies portray karma as a universal law, encouraging individuals to navigate life with mindfulness, compassion, and an awareness of the interconnectedness of all beings.

Purpose of the Book

The purpose of "Living the Karma Way" is to bridge the ancient wisdom of karma with the practicalities of contemporary living, offering readers a transformative roadmap for cultivating a more intentional and harmonious existence. In a world often marked by hectic routines and complex choices, this book seeks to unravel the profound teachings of karma and translate them into actionable steps for personal growth. By exploring the threefold nature of karma, the interconnectedness of actions, and the power of positive intention, this book aims to empower individuals to make conscious choices that align with their values and contribute positively to the world.

Through practical exercises, mindfulness techniques, and insights into responsible living, readers are invited to embark on a journey of self-discovery and personal development, fostering a life rich in compassion, mindfulness, and positive karmic influence. Ultimately, the purpose is to inspire a shift towards a more conscious and fulfilling way of living, guided by the timeless principles of karma.

"Living the Karma Way" is dedicated to exploring the tangible and everyday applications of the profound concept of karma. Beyond a theoretical discourse, this book looks into the nitty-gritty of how individuals can integrate karmic principles into their daily lives, fostering personal growth and positive influence. From cultivating mindful awareness and setting positive intentions to navigating relationships with compassion and embracing responsibility, each chapter offers practical insights and actionable steps.

The aim is to empower readers with a toolkit of transformative practices that extend beyond philosophical contemplation, encouraging the incorporation of karma into one's routine choices, habits, and interactions. By providing real-world examples and applicable strategies, the book aspires to make the ancient wisdom of karma accessible and relevant, demonstrating its potential to bring about positive change in the intricacies of our modern lives.

Cultivating positive habits for a fulfilling existence lies at the heart of "Living the Karma Way." These coming chapters serve as a practical guide for readers seeking to transform their lives by embracing habits that align with positive karmic principles. From the moment we wake to the choices we make throughout the day; our habits shape the fabric of our existence.

This book explores the power of routine, encouraging mindfulness in daily actions, and fostering habits that contribute to personal well-being and the greater good. By encouraging practices such as gratitude, kindness, and self-reflection, readers are empowered to consciously shape their daily rituals, creating a ripple effect that extends beyond individual lives. Through the cultivation of positive habits, this book offers a roadmap to a more fulfilling and harmonious existence, demonstrating how the seemingly small choices we make each day can profoundly influence our journey on the path of karma.

Chapter One: Unraveling the Threads of Karma

Unraveling the threads of Karma serves as the foundational exploration in "Living the Karma Way," shedding light on the intricate dynamics of this ancient and complex concept. This chapter takes readers on a journey through the threefold nature of karma—Sanchita, Prarabdha, and Agami—unpacking the accumulated actions of the past, the current deeds shaping our present, and the seeds we sow for the future. It elucidates how these threads intertwine, illustrating the interconnectedness of our choices and their consequences. By dissecting the essence of cause and effect, this chapter invites contemplation on the role of individual agency in shaping destiny. As readers begin to understand the delicate layers of karma, they gain a deeper understanding of how their actions contribute to the ongoing tapestry of life, empowering them to navigate the complexities of existence with greater awareness and intentionality.

The Three Types of Karma

In the intricate tapestry of karma, understanding the three distinct types—Sanchita, Prarabdha, and Agami—is fundamental to navigating the complexities of life's journey. Sanchita Karma encompasses the accumulated actions from past lives, a reservoir of deeds that shape the current circumstances of an individual. Prarabdha Karma refers to the subset of Sanchita Karma that becomes the current life's destiny, influencing the experiences and challenges one faces in the present. Agami Karma, on the other hand, involves the actions and choices individuals make in the present, shaping the future karmic landscape.

Together, these three dimensions of karma form a dynamic interplay, illustrating the intricate dance of cause and effect that unfolds across time. Through this understanding, readers gain a roadmap for conscious living, recognizing the profound influence of past, present, and future actions on the evolving journey of their lives. Karma, an integral concept in Eastern philosophies, unfolds in three distinct types, each contributing to the intricate dance of cause and effect that shapes our existence.

1. Sanchita Karma (Accumulated Actions): This is the sum total of all actions and deeds from past lives. Often likened to a reservoir, Sanchita Karma represents the accumulated energy of past choices, influencing the conditions of one's current life. It serves as a storehouse of potentialities, waiting to unfold and manifest in various ways as life progresses.

2. Prarabdha Karma (Current Actions): Among the accumulated karma, Prarabdha is the portion chosen to be experienced in the present life. It shapes the current circumstances, challenges, and opportunities an individual encounters. Essentially, Prarabdha Karma represents the destiny chosen for this lifetime, arising from the vast reservoir of Sanchita Karma. It is the thread of fate one weaves into the fabric of their current existence.

3. Agami Karma (Future Actions): Unlike the other two, Agami Karma is the karma created in the present moment. It pertains to the choices and actions individuals make today, influencing their future experiences and shaping the ongoing cycle of cause and effect. Agami Karma emphasizes the significance of conscious decision-making, as it directly impacts the trajectory of one's life and contributes to the reservoir of Sanchita Karma.

Understanding these three types of karma provides a comprehensive view of the dynamic interplay between past, present, and future actions. It offers a roadmap for individuals to navigate their lives with awareness, recognizing the profound influence of their choices on the unfolding journey of existence.

The Interconnectedness of Actions

The concept of karma is intricately woven into the fabric of the interconnectedness of actions, portraying a dynamic and interdependent relationship between our deeds and their consequences. This principle underscores the profound notion that every action, thought, or intention sets forth a series of reactions that reverberate through the intricate web of existence. The interconnectedness of actions highlights that no deed occurs in isolation; instead, each choice contributes to the ongoing tapestry of cause and effect, influencing not only individual destinies but also the collective consciousness.

This understanding invites reflection on the ripple effects of our behaviors, emphasizing the power of conscious living. By acknowledging the interconnectedness of actions, individuals are encouraged to approach life with mindfulness, recognizing the role they play in the grand symphony of existence and fostering a sense of responsibility for the energy they contribute to the world.

In the intricate philosophy of karma, the principle that one action leads to another underscores the dynamic nature of cause and effect. This concept illuminates the idea that each choice, whether significant or seemingly inconsequential, initiates a chain reaction of consequences that shape the course of one's life.

The ripple effect of our choices is a central tenet of the karma philosophy, illustrating how every decision, no matter how small, sends waves through the intricate fabric of existence. Like a stone cast into a tranquil pond, each choice creates concentric circles that expand outward, touching the lives of others and shaping the collective consciousness.

The philosophy of karma teaches us that the consequences of our actions extend far beyond our immediate awareness, influencing the intricate interplay of cause and effect in the grand tapestry of life. Recognizing the ripple effect encourages individuals to approach decision-making with mindfulness, understanding that their choices not only impact their personal journey but also contribute to the well-being of the larger community. This understanding fosters a sense of interconnected responsibility, urging individuals to navigate their lives with a heightened awareness of the enduring impact their choices can have on the world around them.

Chapter Two: Cultivating Mindful Awareness

Much like a domino effect, the repercussions of a single action extend far beyond the immediate moment, influencing subsequent events and experiences. The interconnectedness of actions implies that our deeds create a ripple in the cosmic fabric, setting the stage for the unfolding drama of our existence. This understanding invites individuals to approach their decisions with a heightened sense of awareness, recognizing that the quality of their actions not only molds their personal journey but also contributes to the broader narrative of the collective human experience. In the realm of karma, the recognition that one action leads to another serves as a powerful reminder of the responsibility individuals hold in shaping the trajectory of their lives and the interconnected destiny of all beings.

Cultivating mindful awareness stands as a cornerstone in the practice of living a karma-centered life, inviting individuals to engage with the present moment in a state of non-judgmental awareness. This process involves developing a keen sensitivity to one's thoughts, emotions, and actions, fostering a deep connection with the unfolding reality. Mindful awareness, often cultivated through meditation and contemplative practices, enables individuals to observe the ebb and flow of their inner experiences without attachment or aversion. By being fully present in each moment, one becomes attuned to the interconnected nature of their actions and the consequences they may yield.

This heightened awareness serves as a compass for making conscious choices, aligning personal intentions with the broader tapestry of existence. In essence, the cultivation of mindful awareness empowers individuals to navigate life with clarity and purpose, fostering a harmonious relationship with the ever-changing currents of the present.

Understanding Mindfulness

Understanding mindfulness goes beyond the surface level of a popular buzzword, it teaches a profound state of conscious awareness and presence. Rooted in ancient contemplative practices, mindfulness involves a deliberate and non-judgmental focus on the present moment, encompassing one's thoughts, emotions, and surroundings. It is a mental discipline that encourages individuals to observe their experiences without being consumed by them, fostering a clarity that transcends the chaos of daily life. Through mindfulness, individuals gain insight into the habitual patterns of their minds, promoting a sense of inner balance and tranquility. This heightened awareness enables a deeper understanding of the interconnectedness of all things, aligning actions with intention and fostering a mindful approach to decision-making. Beyond a technique, mindfulness becomes a way of life, transforming routine activities into opportunities for profound insight and fostering a sense of gratitude for the richness of each passing moment.

Mindfulness, at its core, is both a practice and a state of being that involves intentionally paying attention to the present moment with an open and non-judgmental awareness. Rooted in ancient contemplative traditions, mindfulness has gained widespread recognition for its transformative effects on mental well-being and overall quality of life.

The principles of mindfulness revolve around cultivating a heightened awareness of one's thoughts, sensations, and surroundings, fostering an acceptance of the present without undue attachment or aversion. Central to its philosophy is the emphasis on observing the mind's natural tendencies without judgment, allowing for a deep understanding of one's inner experiences. Mindfulness encourages a gentle return to the present when the mind inevitably wanders, promoting a sense of clarity, emotional resilience, and a profound connection to the unfolding reality. As a practice, mindfulness involves various techniques, including meditation, conscious breathing, and mindful movement, all aimed at nurturing a sustained and compassionate attention to the richness of each passing moment.

The benefits of mindfulness in daily life extend across various dimensions, offering a holistic and transformative impact on one's well-being. Embracing mindfulness practices has been linked to reduced stress levels, fostering a sense of calm and resilience in the face of life's challenges. It enhances emotional regulation, promoting a healthier relationship with thoughts and feelings, and reducing symptoms of anxiety and depression. Mindfulness cultivates a heightened awareness of the present moment, leading to improved concentration and cognitive function.

Moreover, the practice encourages a more compassionate and non-reactive attitude towards oneself and others, fostering positive interpersonal relationships. Physiologically, mindfulness has been associated with lower blood pressure, improved immune function, and better overall physical health. As a result, integrating mindfulness into daily life becomes a powerful tool for enhancing mental, emotional, and physical well-being, offering a pathway to a more balanced, intentional, and fulfilling existence.

Practical Techniques for Mindful Living

Practical techniques for mindful living empower individuals to infuse awareness into their daily routines, creating a reservoir of presence that extends beyond formal meditation sessions. Mindful living involves grounding oneself in the current moment amidst the hustle of daily life. Simple yet powerful techniques include mindful breathing, where individuals focus on the rhythm of their breath to anchor their attention to the present.

Incorporating mindful pauses throughout the day allows for a reset, fostering a conscious awareness of thoughts, emotions, and surroundings. Mindful eating encourages savoring each bite, engaging the senses fully in the act of nourishment. Additionally, body scan exercises help individuals connect with physical sensations, promoting relaxation and grounding. By integrating these practical techniques into daily activities, individuals can transform routine moments into opportunities for mindful presence, cultivating a sense of calm, clarity, and purpose in the midst of life's myriad experiences.

Meditation, as a cornerstone of mindfulness, offers a profound journey inward, providing a sanctuary for individuals to cultivate a heightened state of awareness and tranquility. Through various meditation practices, such as focused attention or loving-kindness meditation, individuals learn to observe their thoughts without attachment, fostering a sense of inner calm and clarity. Practice often involves finding a quiet space, adopting a comfortable posture, and directing attention to the breath, a mantra, or specific sensations. Regular meditation has been associated with numerous mental and physical benefits, including stress reduction, improved emotional well-being, and enhanced concentration. As individuals experience the stillness of meditation, they gradually unveil the transformative power of cultivating a mindful presence, paving the way for a more centered and harmonious life.

Mindful breathing and body awareness serve as foundational pillars in the practice of mindfulness, inviting individuals to anchor themselves in the present moment through intentional awareness of the breath and bodily sensations. Mindful breathing involves a gentle focus on inhalation and exhalation, serving as an anchor to the current experience. This practice not only calms the mind but also fosters a deeper connection with the rhythm of life.

Complementing this, body awareness involves consciously directing attention to the sensations present in different parts of the body, promoting a grounded and non-judgmental awareness of the physical self. These practices encourage a profound connection between the mind and body, allowing individuals to cultivate a sense of presence, release tension, and navigate the complexities of daily life with greater clarity and equanimity. By integrating mindful breathing and body awareness into everyday routines, individuals can tap into a wellspring of tranquility and mindfulness that transcends the hectic pace of modern living.

Integrating mindfulness into daily activities transforms the mundane into moments of profound awareness and presence. It involves infusing routine tasks with conscious attention, whether it's sipping a cup of tea, walking, or even washing dishes. Rather than rushing through activities on autopilot, individuals are encouraged to engage their senses fully, savoring the sights, sounds, and sensations of the present moment. By bringing mindful awareness to everyday tasks, individuals cultivate a sense of gratitude, focus, and intentionality. This integration extends beyond formal meditation sessions, allowing for a continuous state of mindfulness throughout the day. It's a practice of being fully engaged in the unfolding tapestry of life, recognizing the sacredness in ordinary moments, and embracing a mindful approach to each step of the journey.

Chapter Three: The Power of Intention

The power of intention lies at the heart of conscious living, weaving a narrative of purpose and direction into the fabric of our actions. Intention serves as the guiding force that shapes the quality and impact of our deeds. By setting positive intentions, individuals align their actions with their values, fostering a sense of meaning and authenticity in their endeavors. The philosophy of karma emphasizes that the purity of intention influences the karmic consequences of an action, underscoring the transformative potential of cultivating positive motives. Whether in relationships, work, or personal growth, the power of intention directs the trajectory of our lives, acting as a compass that steers us towards a more fulfilling and harmonious existence. It encourages individuals to reflect on the motivations behind their choices, fostering a conscious and intentional approach to living that resonates positively with the interconnected web of existence.

Setting Positive Intentions

Setting positive intentions is a transformative practice that empowers individuals to consciously shape the direction of their lives. Intentions act as the guiding compass, directing one's thoughts, choices, and actions toward positive outcomes. By articulating clear and affirming intentions, individuals create a roadmap for personal growth, cultivating a mindset that aligns with their values and aspirations.

In the context of karma, the power of positive intentions is profound, influencing the energy and impact of actions on the intricate tapestry of cause and effect. This practice encourages self-reflection, allowing individuals to explore the deeper motivations behind their goals and decisions. Setting positive intentions becomes a conscious act of co-creation with one's destiny, emphasizing the potential for growth, kindness, and positive contribution to the interconnected web of life.

Aligning actions with positive goals is a conscious and empowering practice that bridges the gap between intention and tangible outcomes.

It involves deliberately directing one's efforts, decisions, and energy toward endeavors that reflect personal values and contribute positively to the surrounding world. By harmonizing actions with positive goals, individuals not only create a roadmap for their own growth but also influence the collective landscape of interconnected experiences.

In the context of karma, this alignment becomes a potent force, shaping the trajectory of one's destiny and contributing to the karmic energy circulating through the universe. It's a deliberate commitment to live in accordance with a set of principles and aspirations, fostering a sense of purpose, fulfillment, and positive impact on the intricate web of cause and effect. Aligning actions with positive goals is an invitation to be intentional architects of our own destiny, molding a life that resonates with authenticity and brings about positive change in the world.

The role of intention in shaping karma is pivotal, highlighting the profound influence of the inner motivations behind our actions on the cosmic fabric of cause and effect. Intentions serve as the seeds from which actions sprout, and in the philosophy of karma, the purity and positivity of these intentions profoundly impact the karmic consequences that unfold.

When actions are guided by benevolent intentions, such as compassion, kindness, and altruism, they contribute positively to the interconnected web of existence. Conversely, actions driven by negative intentions may generate discord and disharmony. Recognizing the significance of intention underscores the transformative potential inherent in cultivating a mindful and virtuous mindset. It prompts individuals to explore the motives behind their choices, encouraging a conscious alignment of actions with positive intentions. In essence, the role of intention in shaping karma emphasizes the power individuals hold to shape their destinies through the intentional cultivation of goodwill, empathy, and positive energy.

Overcoming Negative Intentions

Overcoming negative intentions is a transformative journey towards breaking free from the cycles of harmful thoughts and actions. It involves a conscious effort to acknowledge, confront, and redirect negative impulses that may arise within the mind. The philosophy of karma underscores the significance of this process, recognizing that intentional negativity can contribute to a discordant karmic cycle. By cultivating self-awareness, individuals can dismantle harmful patterns, replacing them with positive intentions rooted in compassion and understanding. This practice fosters personal growth and contributes to the creation of positive energy within the interconnected web of existence. Overcoming negative intentions is an empowering endeavor, highlighting the capacity for self-transformation and the potential to shape a karmic landscape that resonates with harmony, kindness, and positive impact.

Recognizing and transforming harmful intentions is a crucial aspect of the journey toward a more conscious and compassionate existence. It begins with a profound self-awareness that enables individuals to identify negative impulses and intentions that may be at odds with their values. In the realm of karma, this process is pivotal, as it acknowledges the profound impact that harmful intentions can have on the intricate web of cause and effect.

The transformative journey involves a commitment to introspection, understanding the root causes of negative intentions, and consciously choosing to redirect them towards positive alternatives. This practice fosters personal growth and emotional well-being and contributes to the creation of a positive karmic ripple effect. By recognizing and transforming harmful intentions, individuals embark on a powerful path of self-evolution, actively participating in the co-creation of a more harmonious and compassionate reality.

Strategies for fostering positive intentions form a foundational framework for cultivating a mindful and purposeful life. This involves a commitment to self-awareness, encouraging individuals to regularly examine their motivations and redirect their thoughts towards positivity.

Mindfulness practices, such as meditation and conscious breathing, serve as effective strategies to center the mind and align intentions with virtuous principles. Setting clear and achievable goals, both short-term and long-term, provides a roadmap for positive action, helping individuals to stay focused on their values.

Surrounding oneself with a supportive community and engaging in meaningful activities contribute to an environment that nurtures positive intentions. Additionally, embracing a mindset of gratitude and compassion towards oneself and others further reinforces the commitment to fostering positive energy. These strategies collectively empower individuals to navigate life with a conscious intent, contributing to the cultivation of a positive and harmonious karmic landscape.

Chapter Four: Compassion and Empathy

Compassion and empathy, as twin pillars of human connection, form the essence of a karma-centered life. Compassion involves a deep and genuine concern for the well-being of others, accompanied by a heartfelt desire to alleviate their suffering. It is the recognition of shared humanity and interconnectedness, transcending boundaries and fostering a sense of oneness. Empathy, on the other hand, is the ability to understand and share the feelings of another, stepping into their emotional shoes with genuine understanding. Together, these qualities create a powerful synergy that enhances individual well-being and contributes to the positive energy circulating within the broader tapestry of existence.

In the context of karma, acts of compassion and empathy become transformative, generating a ripple effect of kindness, and understanding that reverberates throughout the interconnected web of life. These virtues serve as guiding lights, illuminating a path towards a more harmonious and compassionate world where each action is infused with the intention to alleviate suffering and nurture collective well-being.

Developing a Compassionate Mindset

Developing a compassionate mindset is a transformative endeavor that involves cultivating a deep sense of empathy, understanding, and kindness towards oneself and others. It begins with a commitment to self-awareness, allowing individuals to recognize their own struggles and vulnerabilities with a gentle and non-judgmental attitude.

This self-compassion becomes the foundation for extending empathy to others, fostering an understanding of their experiences and challenges. A compassionate mindset involves actively seeking to alleviate the suffering of those around us, whether through small acts of kindness or more significant gestures of support. In the context of karma, developing a compassionate mindset contributes positively to the interconnected web of existence, creating a ripple effect of goodwill and understanding. This practice enhances personal well-being and plays a vital role in shaping a harmonious and compassionate world. One where each thought and action is imbued with the intention to alleviate suffering and promote collective flourishing.

Compassion, in this philosophical framework, is more than an emotion; it is a transformative force that influences the quality of energy exchanged within the interconnected universe. Acts of kindness and understanding, driven by genuine compassion, contribute positively to the karmic tapestry, fostering a harmonious and benevolent collective reality. Recognizing the shared nature of human experiences and extending compassion towards others influences their well-being and becomes an investment in one's own positive karmic trajectory.

In essence, compassion in the context of karma underscores the interconnectedness of all beings, emphasizing the profound impact that acts of kindness and understanding can have on the evolving narrative of cause and effect in the grand tapestry of life. Practicing self-compassion and extending it to others forms a powerful cycle of benevolence that resonates deeply in the philosophy of karma. Self-compassion involves treating oneself with kindness and understanding, recognizing one's own imperfections without harsh judgment. This practice becomes the cornerstone for fostering empathy and compassion towards others, creating a ripple effect of positive energy. By cultivating self-compassion, individuals develop a reservoir of kindness that naturally extends beyond personal boundaries.

In the intricate dance of cause and effect, acts of self-compassion contribute positively to one's karmic landscape, fostering a mindset of benevolence that influences interpersonal relationships and collective well-being. This reciprocal relationship between self-compassion and compassion towards others illuminates the interconnected nature of human experiences, emphasizing that the kindness we offer ourselves inevitably radiates outward, creating a harmonious resonance within the complex interplay of karma.

Empathy as a Catalyst for Positive Karma

Empathy serves as a catalytic force for positive karma, acting as the bridge that connects individuals in a shared vision of understanding and compassion. In the realm of karma, the ability to genuinely feel and comprehend the experiences of others becomes a transformative influence on the quality of one's actions. Empathy prompts thoughtful consideration of the impact of one's deeds on others, fostering a mindset that prioritizes kindness and benevolence. As individuals extend empathy, stepping into the emotional realms of those around them, they contribute positively to the karmic energy circulating in the universe.

Acts of empathy create a ripple effect, inspiring a chain reaction of understanding and support that transcends individual boundaries. In this way, empathy becomes a catalyst for positive karma, embodying the interconnected nature of human existence and shaping a collective reality that thrives on mutual understanding, kindness, and the harmonious exchange of goodwill.

Cultivating empathy in relationships is a profound journey toward deep connection and understanding. It involves actively listening to others, seeking to comprehend their perspectives and emotions without judgment. By putting oneself in the shoes of a partner, friend, or family member, individuals create a space for shared vulnerability and mutual support. This empathetic approach fosters emotional intimacy, strengthening the bonds between individuals. In the context of karma, cultivating empathy becomes a powerful contributor to positive energy exchange within relationships.

Acts of understanding and kindness create a harmonious dynamic that enhances the well-being of those involved and contributes to the collective positive energy circulating in the interconnected universe. Ultimately, cultivating empathy in relationships becomes a transformative practice, nurturing a shared journey of growth, compassion, and positive karmic influence.

The impact of empathetic actions on karmic balance is profound, as the compassionate energy generated through understanding and kindness contributes positively to personal karma. In the philosophy of karma, empathetic actions create a harmonious resonance, influencing individual destinies and shaping the collective karmic landscape.

When individuals extend empathy, they engage in a cycle of positive reciprocity, fostering an environment of goodwill and understanding. This, in turn, contributes to the creation of positive energy that circulates within the interconnected web of existence. Acts of empathy create a ripple effect, influencing the immediate relationships and echoing throughout the broader network of interconnected lives. By promoting understanding and compassion, empathetic actions become a key player in the delicate balance of karma, fostering a collective reality where positive energy prevails and contributes to the ongoing evolution of the cosmic narrative.

Chapter Five: Embracing Responsibility

Embracing responsibility is a transformative stance that empowers individuals to recognize the impact of their actions. It involves a conscious acknowledgment of the consequences that arise from one's choices and a commitment to take ownership of both the positive and challenging outcomes. In the context of karma, embracing responsibility becomes a fundamental principle, as it aligns with the understanding that every action sets forth a chain of cause and effect. This practice goes beyond mere accountability; it encourages individuals to actively shape their destinies by making mindful choices and cultivating positive intentions. Embracing responsibility fosters a sense of agency, urging individuals to contribute positively to their own lives and collective well-being. It becomes a transformative force, guiding individuals towards a more intentional and harmonious existence where actions are rooted in awareness, accountability, and a deep understanding of the interconnected nature of all things.

Taking Ownership of Actions

Taking ownership of actions is a powerful commitment to accountability and personal growth. It involves a conscious acknowledgment of the choices one makes and an acceptance of the responsibility that comes with those decisions. This practice goes hand in hand with the principles of karma, recognizing that each action sets forth a series of consequences that shape one's journey.

By taking ownership, individuals move beyond blame or avoidance and embrace a proactive role in shaping their destinies. This self-awareness allows for introspection and learning from both successes and setbacks. Taking ownership of actions becomes a transformative process, empowering individuals to navigate life with intentionality and contribute positively to the interconnected tapestry of cause and effect. Ultimately, this practice is about recognizing the consequences of past actions and actively influencing the future by making mindful and responsible choices in the present.

Acknowledging the consequences of choices is an integral step in the journey toward self-awareness and responsible living. It involves a conscious recognition that every decision, whether significant or seemingly minor, sets forth a chain of events that reverberates through one's life. This practice aligns with the principles of karma, emphasizing the cause-and-effect nature of actions. By acknowledging consequences, individuals gain insight into the ripple effects of their choices, fostering a heightened awareness of the impact on themselves and the world around them. It's a reflective process that invites a deeper understanding of the interconnected nature of existence. In doing so, individuals take responsibility for their actions while gaining the wisdom to make more mindful and intentional choices, contributing positively to their own growth and the broader karmic landscape.

Learning from mistakes and evolving is a fundamental aspect of personal growth and resilience. It involves a conscious effort to glean insights and understanding from past errors, using them as steppingstones toward improvement and self-discovery. Embracing the philosophy of karma, this practice aligns with the notion that each mistake carries valuable lessons and contributes to the ongoing narrative of cause and effect. By acknowledging mistakes without judgment, individuals create space for self-reflection and growth.

Learning from these experiences not only builds wisdom but also cultivates a mindset of adaptability and resilience. In the grand tapestry of life, the ability to evolve from mistakes becomes a transformative force, guiding individuals toward a more enlightened and intentional existence where the journey is marked not only by successes but also by the invaluable lessons gained from setbacks.

Resolving Karmic Debt

Resolving karmic debt involves a conscious and intentional effort to address the consequences of past actions and bring about positive change. In the philosophy of karma, it is believed that actions from the past, whether positive or negative, create an energetic imprint that influences future experiences. To resolve karmic debt, individuals embark on a journey of self-awareness, acknowledging and taking responsibility for their past actions.

This process often involves acts of kindness, forgiveness, and making amends where possible. By cultivating positive intentions and engaging in actions that contribute positively to the interconnected web of existence, individuals strive to balance the karmic scales. The resolution of karmic debt is a transformative journey that encourages personal growth, compassion, and a mindful approach to decision-making, ultimately shaping a more harmonious and intentional life path.

Strategies for resolving past negative karma involve a multifaceted and intentional approach to cultivating positive change and personal growth. Begin with honest self-reflection, acknowledging past actions and their consequences without judgment. Embrace a mindset of accountability and take proactive steps to make amends where possible, seeking forgiveness and understanding. Engage in acts of kindness and compassion, both towards yourself and others, to generate positive energy. Cultivate mindfulness in decision-making, ensuring that present actions align with positive intentions.

Consistent self-improvement through learning from mistakes contributes to breaking negative karmic cycles. Seek guidance from spiritual or ethical mentors and consider engaging in practices that promote inner balance and positive energy. Remember that the journey to resolve negative karma is ongoing, requiring patience, perseverance, and a commitment to living in accordance with principles of kindness and understanding.

Making amends and seeking forgiveness is a profound and transformative process that requires introspection, humility, and genuine remorse. It involves acknowledging the impact of past actions on others, taking full responsibility for any harm caused, and actively working to repair relationships. A crucial component is offering a sincere apology, expressing remorse without justification, and understanding the perspectives of those affected. Making amends goes beyond words, requiring concrete actions that demonstrate commitment to positive change and personal growth.

Simultaneously, seeking forgiveness involves understanding that forgiveness is a process, not an immediate outcome, and respecting the autonomy of those who have been hurt. It's a journey of empathy, healing, and rebuilding trust. When we contribute to individual growth and the fostering of compassion and understanding within an interconnected human relationship, both individuals will have a positive outcome.

Chapter Six: Detoxifying the Mind and Body

Detoxifying the mind and body is a holistic approach to promoting overall well-being and balance. In the realm of mental wellness, it involves clearing the mind of negativity, stress, and clutter through practices such as meditation, mindfulness, and positive affirmations. These practices aim to cultivate mental clarity, emotional resilience, and a more positive outlook. On the physical front, detoxification often involves adopting healthy lifestyle choices, including a nutritious diet, regular exercise, and adequate hydration. By eliminating or minimizing exposure to toxins and embracing nourishing habits, the body's natural detoxification processes are supported. The complexity of the mind and body underscores the importance of a comprehensive approach to detoxification, fostering a harmonious and balanced state that contributes to overall health and vitality.

The Connection Between Physical and Mental Health

The connection between physical and mental health is intricate and undeniable. The two are deeply interlinked, with each exerting a profound influence on the other. Physical health significantly impacts mental well-being, as factors such as nutrition, exercise, and sleep play crucial roles in regulating mood, cognitive function, and emotional resilience. Conversely, mental health has tangible effects on the body, influencing physiological processes and immune function.

Stress, anxiety, or depression, for instance, can manifest physically through symptoms like headaches, digestive issues, or muscle tension. Recognizing this mind-body connection emphasizes the importance of a holistic approach to health, where caring for both physical and mental aspects is essential for overall well-being. Nurturing this symbiotic relationship through practices like regular exercise, mindfulness, and a balanced lifestyle contributes to a harmonious and integrated state of health.

Holistic well-being, encompassing the interconnected dimensions of physical, mental, and spiritual health, is integral to the philosophy of karma. It acknowledges that each facet of well-being contributes to the intricate web of cause and effect, shaping one's karmic journey. Nurturing physical health through mindful living, exercise, and a balanced diet fosters positive energy that reverberates through the universe. Mental well-being, achieved through practices like meditation and positive mindset, influences the quality of intentions and actions, thereby influencing karmic consequences.

The spiritual dimension, involving a sense of purpose and connection to a greater whole, aligns actions with higher values, contributing positively to the collective karmic tapestry. Holistic well-being, therefore, becomes a personal pursuit and a conscious interconnected contribution to the harmonious flow of energy in the cosmic dance of positive karma.

Maintaining a healthy mind and body involves a combination of mindful practices that address both mental and physical well-being. Regular exercise, such as cardiovascular activities, strength training, or yoga, contributes to physical health by enhancing cardiovascular fitness, muscle strength, and flexibility. A nutritious and well-balanced diet provides the essential nutrients for overall health, supporting both physical and mental functions. Prioritizing sufficient sleep is crucial, as it allows the body to regenerate and promotes cognitive functioning.

Mindfulness and meditation practices foster mental well-being by reducing stress, improving focus, and cultivating a sense of inner calm. Regular self-reflection and journaling can be valuable for maintaining emotional health, fostering self-awareness and resilience. Additionally, engaging in hobbies, spending time in nature, and cultivating positive social connections contribute to a holistic approach to well-being, nurturing both the mind and body.

Letting Go of Toxic Habits

Letting go of toxic habits is a transformative process that involves intentional self-reflection, determination, and a commitment to positive change. It begins with identifying and acknowledging habits that contribute to negative outcomes in one's life. Whether these habits are related to unhealthy relationships, self-destructive behaviors, or patterns that hinder personal growth, recognizing their toxicity is the first step.

Next comes a conscious decision to break free from these habits, often requiring changes in mindset, routine, and environment. Establishing healthier alternatives and support systems can aid in this process. Practicing self-compassion and patience is crucial, as breaking toxic habits is rarely a linear journey. Embracing personal growth, seeking professional help if needed, and surrounding oneself with a positive and understanding community contribute to the transformative process of letting go of toxic habits. Ultimately, it's about reclaiming agency over one's life and fostering a positive and nurturing environment for personal development.

Identifying and releasing negative patterns is a crucial step toward personal growth and well-being. It involves a mindful examination of recurrent behaviors, thoughts, or reactions that contribute to undesired outcomes. Self-awareness plays a key role in this process, as individuals need to recognize when these negative patterns manifest and the impact they have on their lives. Once identified, the next step is to understand the underlying triggers and motivations behind these patterns. This self-reflection provides insight into the root causes, enabling individuals to address and release these negative tendencies. Strategies for releasing negative patterns may include adopting new, positive habits, seeking support from friends or professionals, and cultivating a mindset of self-compassion and resilience. The journey to release negative patterns is an ongoing process that involves commitment, patience, and a genuine desire for personal transformation.

Nurturing positive habits is a fundamental aspect of cultivating a karmically balanced life. It involves consciously integrating habits that contribute positively to one's well-being and the interconnected web of existence. Mindful practices, such as meditation and gratitude exercises, foster a positive mindset and contribute to mental well-being. Engaging in regular physical activity enhances physical health and generates positive energy that aligns with the principles of karma. Cultivating kindness, empathy, and compassion in daily interactions with others creates a ripple effect of positive energy in the collective karmic tapestry.

Establishing habits of self-care, including adequate sleep, a balanced diet, and stress management, heals the body and mind. The intention behind these positive habits is crucial, as it shapes the energy that emanates from one's actions, influencing the karmic consequences. By consistently nurturing positive habits, individuals contribute to a more harmonious and karmically balanced life.

Chapter Seven: Building Positive Relationships

Building positive relationships is a transformative process that involves intentional effort, empathy, and effective communication. It begins with cultivating self-awareness, understanding one's values, and recognizing the importance of healthy connections. Authenticity is key, as individuals contribute to positive relationships by being genuine and true to themselves. Active listening, a cornerstone of effective communication, fosters understanding and strengthens emotional bonds. Expressing gratitude and appreciation further nurtures positivity within relationships, creating a reciprocal atmosphere of support and kindness.

Resolving conflicts with compassion and a willingness to compromise is crucial for maintaining positive connections. Additionally, setting healthy boundaries ensures that relationships remain respectful and balanced. Ultimately, building positive relationships is an ongoing journey that requires commitment, open-mindedness, and a genuine investment in the well-being of oneself and others.

The Influence of Relationships on Karma

Relationships play a profound role in the intricate dance of karma, influencing the energy that flows through the interconnected web of existence. Positive relationships, built on trust, empathy, and mutual respect, contribute to the generation of harmonious karmic energy.

Acts of kindness, understanding, and support within relationships create positive ripples that extend beyond individuals, impacting the collective karmic landscape. Conversely, negative relationships, characterized by conflict, toxicity, or harm, introduce discordant energy into the karmic tapestry. The intentions and actions within relationships become either positive or negative experiences. Recognizing the influence of relationships on karma underscores the importance of cultivating healthy connections, as the energy exchanged within these dynamics shapes individual destinies and contributes to the overall balance and harmony of one's karma.

The dynamics of interpersonal karma encompass the complex interplay of intentions, actions, and consequences within the realm of relationships. In essence, interpersonal karma reflects the energy exchange and impact that individuals have on each other's lives. Positive intentions, such as love, compassion, and support, contribute to a harmonious karmic energy that nurtures the well-being of those involved. Acts of kindness and understanding within relationships create a positive ripple effect that extends beyond individual interactions. Conversely, negative intentions, such as resentment, betrayal, or harm, introduce discordant energy into the karmic tapestry, influencing the destinies of those involved.

The quality of interpersonal karma is deeply influenced by the choices individuals make in their relationships, emphasizing the significance of mindful actions, empathy, and positive communication. Recognizing and understanding the dynamics of interpersonal karma encourages a conscious and intentional approach to cultivating harmonious connections, contributing positively to the broader web of cause and effect.

Nurturing positive connections while letting go of toxic ones is a transformative process that involves intentional choices and self-care. Cultivating positive connections entails surrounding oneself with individuals who uplift, support, and contribute positively to one's well-being. These relationships are characterized by trust, mutual respect, and shared values. Actively investing time and energy into these connections creates a harmonious karmic exchange, fostering a positive atmosphere that extends beyond individual interactions.

Conversely, recognizing and letting go of toxic relationships is an essential step in maintaining a karmically balanced life. Toxic connections, marked by negativity, manipulation, or harm, introduce discordant energy into one's life. Releasing these relationships involves setting boundaries, prioritizing self-care, and making choices that align with personal growth and well-being. While the process might be challenging, the act of letting go contributes to the creation of a more positive and balanced karmic landscape. Ultimately, nurturing positive connections and letting go of toxic ones is a dynamically intentional practice that shapes the quality of relationships and influences the broader understanding of consequences.

Communication Skills for Harmonious Relationships

Effective communication is a cornerstone for building and sustaining harmonious relationships. Effective communication can directly affect a positive or negative experience. Understanding both sides of the mutual narrative is key to developing a meaningful relationship.

Here are key communication skills that contribute to positive connections:

Active Listening: Demonstrate genuine interest in what others are saying. Practice active listening by giving your full attention, making eye contact, and providing feedback to show that you understand.

Empathy: Cultivate empathy by trying to understand others' perspectives and feelings. This fosters a deeper connection and mutual understanding within the relationship.

Clear Expression: Articulate your thoughts and feelings clearly and honestly. Avoid assumptions and be specific about your needs, expectations, and boundaries.

Open-Mindedness: Approach conversations with an open mind. Be willing to consider different viewpoints and avoid judgment or defensiveness.

Non-Verbal Communication: Pay attention to non-verbal cues, such as body language and tone of voice. These aspects can convey emotions and intentions that may not be expressed verbally.

Effective Feedback: Provide constructive feedback in a respectful and constructive manner. Focus on specific behaviors rather than generalizing about the person.

Conflict Resolution: Develop skills for resolving conflicts peacefully. Use "I" statements to express your feelings and work collaboratively to find mutually acceptable solutions.

Patience and Timing: Practice patience and choose the right timing for important conversations. Avoid discussing sensitive topics when emotions are heightened.

Positive Reinforcement: Acknowledge and appreciate positive behaviors in others. Positive reinforcement strengthens the connection and encourages healthy communication patterns.

Mindful Communication: Practice mindfulness in communication by being fully present in the moment. Avoid distractions and engage in conversations with focused attention.

Adaptability: Be adaptable in your communication style. Recognize and respect the diversity in communication preferences among individuals and adjust your approach accordingly.

Cultivating these communication skills enhances the quality of interactions, promotes understanding, and contributes to the creation of harmonious relationships within the context of the intricate karmic dynamics at play.

Active listening is a fundamental component of effective communication and plays a crucial role in fostering understanding, building trust, and creating harmonious relationships.

Here are key aspects of active listening and how they contribute to effective communication:

Full Attention: Active listening involves giving your full attention to the speaker. Put away distractions, make eye contact, and show that you are fully present in the conversation.

Non-Verbal Cues: Use non-verbal cues such as nodding, smiling, and maintaining an open posture to convey attentiveness and encouragement. These cues signal to the speaker that you are engaged and receptive.

Avoiding Interruptions: Allow the speaker to express themselves without interruption. Avoid finishing their sentences or interjecting your thoughts prematurely, as this demonstrates respect for their perspective.

Reflective Responses: Provide reflective responses to show that you are actively processing the information. This can involve paraphrasing what the speaker said or summarizing key points to confirm your understanding.

Clarifying Questions: Ask clarifying questions to ensure you fully grasp the speaker's message. This demonstrates a genuine interest in understanding their perspective and encourages open dialogue.

Empathy: Actively engage with the speaker's emotions and try to understand their feelings. Expressing empathy fosters a deeper connection and contributes to a supportive communication environment.

Withholding Judgment: Suspend judgment and avoid forming opinions prematurely. Active listening requires an open mind, allowing for a more complete understanding of the speaker's thoughts and feelings.

Patience: Practice patience, especially in complex or emotionally charged conversations. Give the speaker the time they need to express themselves fully.

Responding Appropriately: Respond thoughtfully and considerately. Tailor your responses to the speaker's communication style and be mindful of the impact your words may have on the overall conversation.

Reciprocal Nature: Recognize that effective communication is a reciprocal process. Encourage the speaker to actively listen to your perspective, creating a balanced and respectful exchange.

In the context of karma and relationship dynamics, active listening contributes to positive energy exchange. By valuing and understanding the perspectives of others, individuals can cultivate a karmically balanced environment that promotes mutual respect and harmony.

Resolving conflicts with compassion and understanding is a transformative process that involves approaching disagreements with a mindful and empathetic mindset. The key elements include emotional regulation, active listening, and expressing empathy to foster a deeper understanding of each party's perspective. Using "I" statements and avoiding blame shifts the focus to the issue at hand rather than individual accusations.

Seeking common ground and collaborating on solutions promotes a sense of shared responsibility and mutual benefit. Apologizing and forgiving, when appropriate, contributes to closure and reconciliation. Embracing conflicts as opportunities for learning and growth, and establishing clear boundaries, further supports a karmically balanced environment where positive intentions and actions prevail. This approach aligns with principles of respect, empathy, and collaboration, creating a foundation for stronger and more harmonious relationships.

Chapter Eight: Living in Harmony with Nature

Living in harmony with nature involves embracing practices and attitudes that foster a respectful and sustainable coexistence with the environment. This holistic approach encourages environmental stewardship, emphasizing the interconnectedness between humans and the natural world. Key principles include conservation of natural resources, mindful consumption, and a deep connection with nature through outdoor activities. Protecting biodiversity, reducing waste, making ethical food choices, and opting for green transportation are essential components. Environmental education, community engagement, and a mindful, respectful attitude toward nature contribute to the overall goal of creating a healthier planet and promoting a balanced and harmonious relationship between humanity and the Earth.

The Ecological Aspect of Karma

The ecological aspect of karma extends beyond individual actions to encompass the collective impact of human behavior on the environment. In this context, karma reflects the interconnected relationship between human actions and the health of the planet. Positive environmental karma involves mindful practices that contribute to the well-being of ecosystems, such as sustainable living, conservation efforts, and a reduced ecological footprint. Conversely, negative environmental karma is generated through activities that harm nature, such as pollution, deforestation, and overconsumption.

Understanding the ecological aspect of karma underscores the responsibility individuals bear for the health of the Earth, emphasizing the importance of sustainable choices and environmental stewardship to create positive energy within the intricate web of cause and effect that binds humanity to the natural world.

Recognizing the interconnectedness of all living things is an acknowledgment of the profound and intricate web of relationships that binds every element of existence. It is an understanding that extends beyond individual boundaries, emphasizing the interdependence of humans, animals, plants, and the entire ecosystem. This awareness highlights that the well-being of one species is intricately linked to the health of others and the overall balance of nature. Whether through ecological systems, shared resources, or the delicate balance of ecosystems, the recognition of interconnectedness invites a sense of responsibility and reverence for all life. It underscores the profound truth that the actions of one being, no matter how small, have the potential to reverberate across the interconnected tapestry of existence, shaping the collective destiny of all living things.

Sustainable living practices are the cornerstone of positive environmental karma, embodying a conscious and responsible approach to daily life that respects the Earth's finite resources. Embracing a minimalist mindset, individuals can reduce their ecological footprint by adopting practices such as conserving energy, water, and resources, as well as minimizing waste through recycling and composting.

Choosing eco-friendly and locally sourced products, supporting renewable energy sources, and opting for green transportation contribute to a positive environmental impact. Sustainable living extends beyond individual actions to encompass community engagement, environmental advocacy, and a commitment to fostering awareness. By making mindful choices aligned with ecological sustainability, individuals create a harmonious relationship with the environment and promote a balanced karmic energy within the intricate tapestry of life.

Mindful Consumption

Mindful consumption is a conscious and intentional approach to the way we acquire and utilize goods and services, emphasizing awareness and responsibility throughout the entire consumption process. It involves making choices that consider the environmental, social, and ethical implications of our purchases. Practicing mindful consumption means opting for products with sustainable and eco-friendly attributes, supporting businesses that prioritize ethical practices, and choosing quality over quantity. By understanding the impact of our consumption patterns on the broader ecosystem and global communities, we can contribute to positive change. Mindful consumption aligns with the principle of being present and aware of the consequences of our actions, fostering a karmically balanced relationship with those actions and consequences.

Making ethical choices in daily life involves a conscientious and deliberate approach to decision-making that considers the moral implications of one's actions. It encompasses a commitment to principles such as honesty, integrity, empathy, and social responsibility. Ethical choices extend to various aspects of life, including personal relationships, professional conduct, and interactions with the broader community. Individuals who prioritize ethical decision-making often strive to minimize harm, promote fairness and justice, and contribute positively to the well-being of others. By aligning actions with ethical values, individuals shape their own character and contribute to the creation of a more compassionate and just society. In the context of karma, making ethical choices reflects an understanding of the interconnectedness of all actions and their potential impact on our existence.

Reducing the ecological footprint through conscious living involves making intentional choices that minimize one's impact on the environment. It requires a thoughtful examination of daily habits, resource consumption, and lifestyle practices. Conscious living encompasses actions such as reducing energy and water consumption, adopting sustainable transportation methods, and minimizing waste through recycling and reusing. Choosing locally sourced and eco-friendly products, as well as embracing a plant-based diet, further contributes to lowering the ecological footprint. This approach involves a mindset of mindfulness and responsibility, recognizing the interconnectedness between individual choices and the health of the planet.

By consciously aligning actions with environmental sustainability, individuals can play a vital role in preserving the Earth's resources and fostering positive energy within the intricate web of cause and effect that defines our ecological impact.

Chapter Nine: Using Karma to Connect with the Universe

The concept of karma serves as a profound gateway to connecting with the universe on a spiritual and cosmic level. At its core, karma is the law of cause and effect, suggesting that our actions, intentions, and thoughts create a ripple effect that reverberates not only through our personal lives but also through the vast expanse of the universe. To utilize karma as a means of connection with the universe is to recognize that we are not isolated beings, but integral threads woven into the intricate tapestry of existence.

Karma operates on the principle that our actions carry energy, and this energy, whether positive or negative, becomes a part of the universal flow. Every act of kindness, compassion, and love contributes to the positive energy circulating within the cosmos, creating a harmonious resonance that extends far beyond individual boundaries. Conversely, actions rooted in negativity or harm introduce discordant notes into this cosmic symphony.

Connecting with the universe through karma involves a heightened awareness of our actions and their inherent consequences. It is an invitation to cultivate mindfulness in every thought, word, and deed, recognizing that each contributes to the cosmic dance of cause and effect. By aligning our actions with positive intentions and ethical choices, we shape our immediate destinies and actively participate in the co-creation of a more balanced and harmonious universe.

Mindfulness, a cornerstone of karma philosophy, becomes a powerful tool for connecting with the universe. Through mindfulness, we become attuned to the present moment, acknowledging the intricate interplay of energies within and around us. This heightened awareness allows us to navigate life with greater clarity, making choices that resonate positively with the universal energy field. In this state of mindfulness, we tap into the universal consciousness, feeling the interconnectedness that binds all living things.

Meditation becomes a profound practice for harnessing the energies of karma and deepening our connection with the universe. In the stillness of meditation, we observe the fluctuations of our thoughts and emotions, gaining insight into the subtle energies that influence our actions. Through regular meditation, we learn to quiet the mind, allowing us to attune ourselves to the cosmic vibrations that permeate the universe. This attunement facilitates a deeper understanding of the interconnected web of karma, as we become conscious co-creators of cosmic energy.

Karma, as a cosmic connector, extends beyond the realm of individual actions to encompass collective energies. The choices made by communities, societies, and humanity contribute to the vibrational frequency of the universe. To use karma to connect with the universe is to recognize the collective responsibility we share in shaping the energy that permeates the cosmos. Conscious efforts towards creating positive change on a global scale, fostering compassion, and promoting sustainability all become integral aspects of contributing to cosmic harmony.

The practice of gratitude becomes a potent way to connect with the universe through karma. By expressing gratitude for the abundance in our lives, we attune ourselves to the flow of positive energy. Gratitude serves as a magnetic force, drawing in more of what we appreciate and aligning us with the universal abundance that surrounds us. In the karmic sense, the energy of gratitude echoes through the universe, creating a reciprocal flow of positive energy.

The principle of interconnectedness, inherent in karma philosophy, emphasizes that every being and element in the universe is interconnected. To connect with the universe through karma is to honor this interconnected web of life. This involves recognizing the inherent value and interconnectedness of all living things, fostering compassion and empathy towards every being. By treating others with kindness and respect, we actively contribute to the positive energy circulating in the universe, fostering a sense of unity that transcends individual boundaries.

Synchronicity, often considered a manifestation of cosmic alignment, becomes a fascinating aspect of connecting with the universe through karma. As we align our actions with positive intentions and cultivate mindfulness, we become more attuned to the subtle signs and synchronicities that the universe presents. These meaningful coincidences serve as affirmations that our energies are in harmony with the cosmic flow, guiding us along a path that resonates with our higher purpose.

To connect with the universe through karma is to embrace the idea that challenges and setbacks are opportunities for growth and transformation. When faced with adversity, viewing it through the lens of karma allows us to understand that our present circumstances are influenced by past actions. By approaching challenges with resilience, humility, and a commitment to positive change, we actively participate in the cosmic dance of cause and effect, steering the trajectory of our karma towards a more enlightened and harmonious existence.

Environmental stewardship emerges as a natural extension of connecting with the universe through karma. Recognizing that our actions impact the delicate balance of the Earth's ecosystems, individuals who align with the principles of karma become advocates for sustainable living and environmental conservation. By cultivating an awareness of our ecological footprint and making choices that minimize harm to the planet, we contribute to the positive energy circulating in the universe and actively participate in the cosmic dance of environmental harmony.

The concept of reincarnation, intertwined with karma in many philosophical traditions, introduces the idea that our connection with the universe transcends the boundaries of a single lifetime. To connect with the universe through karma is to understand that the energies we set into motion endure and continue to shape our spiritual evolution across lifetimes. This realization inspires a sense of responsibility towards our own spiritual growth and the collective evolution of consciousness.

In essence, using karma to connect with the universe is a holistic approach to living that goes beyond individual actions and embraces a cosmic perspective. It invites us to be conscious co-creators in the grand tapestry of existence, recognizing that our energies contribute to the universal symphony of cause and effect. Through mindfulness, meditation, gratitude, and ethical living, we attune ourselves to the cosmic vibrations that surround us, fostering a deep and meaningful connection with the universe. As we navigate the intricate dance of karma, we become active participants in the cosmic flow, weaving our destinies into the vast fabric of the cosmos.

Chapter Ten: Connecting to the Bodhisattva

Connecting to the Bodhisattva is a profound exploration into the heart of Mahayana Buddhist philosophy, a path that transcends personal enlightenment and compassionately embraces the welfare of all sentient beings. At its core, the term "Bodhisattva" is composed of two Sanskrit words: "Bodhi," meaning enlightenment, and "Sattva," meaning sentient being (Awakening Spirit). The Bodhisattva embodies the altruistic spirit of awakening, dedicating their existence to the alleviation of suffering for the benefit of others. This concept finds its roots in the teachings of Siddhartha Gautama, the historical Buddha, who, upon attaining enlightenment under the Bodhi tree, faced a pivotal choice — to enter Nirvana and liberate himself from the cycle of rebirth or to remain in the world to guide others toward enlightenment.

The Bodhisattva ideal, central to Mahayana Buddhism, envisions a journey beyond personal salvation to a selfless commitment to the well-being and enlightenment of all beings. It is an ethos that transcends individual liberation, reflecting the boundless compassion and wisdom inherent in those who tread the Bodhisattva path. Understanding the Bodhisattva involves delving into the multifaceted dimensions of this noble aspiration, encompassing compassion, wisdom, and the six paramitas or perfections that guide the Bodhisattva's conduct.

Compassion, the foundational virtue of the Bodhisattva, radiates as a boundless, all-encompassing love that extends to every sentient being, without discrimination or limitation. The Bodhisattva's heart is an inexhaustible wellspring of compassion, stirred by the recognition of the universal nature of suffering. This profound empathy propels the Bodhisattva to actively engage with the world, to alleviate suffering wherever it is found. Compassion in the Bodhisattva path is not a passive sentiment but a dynamic force that propels selfless action and the cultivation of qualities that benefit others.

Wisdom, the second pillar of the Bodhisattva path, complements compassion, providing the discernment needed to address the root causes of suffering. It involves seeing beyond the surface of phenomena and understanding the interconnected and impermanent nature of reality. Wisdom enables the Bodhisattva to navigate the complexities of existence with clarity, offering insights that guide compassionate action. The synthesis of compassion and wisdom is often symbolized by the Bodhisattva Avalokiteshvara, whose thousand eyes represent the all-seeing nature of wisdom, while the thousand arms symbolize the myriad ways compassion can manifest in the world.

The Bodhisattva's commitment to perfection finds expression in the six paramitas, virtues that shape their conduct and guide their spiritual evolution. These perfections are generosity (dana), ethical conduct (shila), patience (kshanti), diligence (virya), meditation (dhyana), and wisdom (prajna). Each paramita represents a facet of the Bodhisattva's character, honed through dedicated practice for the benefit of all sentient beings.

Generosity, the first paramita, extends beyond material offerings to include the giving of one's time, attention, and compassion. The Bodhisattva, embodying the spirit of selfless giving, recognizes that the act of generosity transcends the donor, the recipient, and the gift itself. It becomes an expression of interconnectedness and an antidote to the self-centered attachments that perpetuate suffering.

Ethical conduct, the second paramita, is the cornerstone of the Bodhisattva's path. Grounded in compassion and wisdom, ethical conduct involves aligning one's actions with the principles of non-harming and benefiting others. The Bodhisattva engages in a continuous process of refining their conduct, recognizing that ethical behavior is a gateway to spiritual growth and a foundation for cultivating a compassionate society.

Patience, the third paramita, is a quality that enables the Bodhisattva to remain steadfast in the face of challenges. It involves enduring adversity with equanimity, cultivating a serene acceptance of the inevitable ups and downs of life. Patience is not passive resignation but an active quality that allows the Bodhisattva to respond to difficulties with wisdom and compassion.

Diligence, the fourth paramita, is the unwavering commitment to spiritual practice and the pursuit of awakening. It involves the enthusiastic and persistent effort to overcome obstacles and cultivate positive qualities. Diligence empowers the Bodhisattva to navigate the complexities of the path, inspiring them to persevere in the face of adversity and distractions.

Meditation, the fifth paramita, is the transformative practice that leads to a direct experience of reality. The Bodhisattva engages in meditation not as a solitary pursuit but as a means of deepening their understanding of the interconnected nature of existence. Meditation becomes a powerful tool for cultivating mindfulness, concentration, and insight, nurturing the Bodhisattva's spiritual evolution.

Wisdom, the sixth paramita, is the culmination of the Bodhisattva's journey. It involves the direct realization of the nature of reality and the transcendence of dualistic thinking. Wisdom is not confined to intellectual understanding but is an experiential knowledge that cuts through the veils of ignorance. This profound insight liberates the Bodhisattva from the cycle of suffering and empowers them to guide others toward enlightenment.

The Bodhisattva's journey unfolds within the framework of the Six Realms of Existence, a symbolic representation of the different states of consciousness within the cycle of birth and death. The Bodhisattva, motivated by compassion, aspires to traverse these realms to assist beings in their quest for liberation. This journey involves a continuous cycle of birth and rebirth, with each incarnation offering opportunities for the Bodhisattva to refine their qualities and deepen their understanding.

Understanding the Bodhisattva also requires exploring the bodhicitta, the awakened mind that embodies the Bodhisattva's compassionate and enlightened intention. Bodhicitta arises from the recognition that the well-being of others is inseparable from one's own liberation. There are two aspects of bodhicitta — relative and ultimate. Relative bodhicitta involves cultivating the aspiration for enlightenment for the benefit of all beings, while ultimate bodhicitta is the direct realization of the nature of reality, transcending concepts of self and other.

The Bodhisattva's journey is vividly illustrated in the Avatamsaka Sutra, a foundational text in the Mahayana tradition. This sutra describes the vast and interconnected nature of reality, portraying the Bodhisattva as a compassionate being who skillfully engages with the world to uplift others. The imagery of the net of Indra, woven with jewels that reflect one another, illustrates the interconnectedness of all phenomena and beings.

The Bodhisattva's compassion extends even to those who may act as adversaries or obstacles on the path. Rather than harboring resentment or aversion, the Bodhisattva responds with equanimity and skillful means. This attitude is embodied in the practice of tonglen, a Tibetan meditation technique where the practitioner breathes in the suffering of others and breathes out compassion and relief.

The Bodhisattva's journey is not without challenges. The Bodhisattvic path demands a radical shift in perspective — a transcendence of ego-centric concerns in favor of the welfare of others. It requires confronting the illusion of separateness and embracing the interconnectedness of all beings. This shift, known as the "turning of the Dharma wheel," is a pivotal moment in the Bodhisattva's journey when they commit to the path of selfless service.

The Bodhisattva, motivated by boundless compassion, engages in skillful means (upaya) to benefit beings according to their needs and capacities. This may involve teachings, acts of kindness, or even taking on specific forms to connect with diverse beings. Skillful means exemplify the adaptability and creative compassion of the Bodhisattva, who tailors their approach to the unique circumstances of each being.

The Bodhisattva's engagement with the world is not detached or aloof but deeply compassionate and intimately connected. They immerse themselves in the human experience, understanding the intricacies of joy, suffering, and the myriad emotions that characterize sentient existence. This empathetic connection allows the Bodhisattva to respond with genuine understanding and guide others toward the path of liberation.

The culmination of the Bodhisattva's journey is the attainment of Buddhahood, the state of perfect enlightenment. The Bodhisattva, having traversed the path with unwavering compassion and wisdom, becomes a fully awakened being, free from the cycle of birth and death. However, the Bodhisattva's commitment to the welfare of others remains, as they manifest in various forms to guide beings along the path of enlightenment.

In conclusion, understanding the Bodhisattva is an exploration into the altruistic heart of Mahayana Buddhism, where the quest for personal enlightenment seamlessly intertwines with the compassionate commitment to the welfare of all sentient beings. The Bodhisattva's path, characterized by boundless compassion, wisdom, and the six paramitas, offers a profound template for navigating the complexities of existence. It invites individuals to transcend the confines of self-centered concerns, embracing a universal perspective that recognizes the interconnectedness of all life. The Bodhisattva, embodying the awakened mind and aspiring to Buddhahood, beckons humanity toward a path of selfless service, compassion, and the ultimate realization of the oneness that pervades the cosmos.

Chapter Eleven: Mindful Conclusion

In conscious reasoning, "Living the Karma Way" offers a comprehensive roadmap for individuals seeking a more mindful and purposeful existence. The journey begins with a deep exploration of the karma concept, understanding its historical, cultural, and philosophical roots. The purpose of the book becomes clear—to empower readers to cultivate positive habits, unravel the threads of karma, and navigate the intricacies of cause and effect in their daily lives.

From exploring the three types of karma to delving into the interconnectedness of actions, the book emphasizes the transformative power of mindful awareness. It guides readers through practical techniques, including meditation practices and strategies for fostering positive intentions. Moreover, the book underscores the importance of compassion, empathy, and responsible decision-making in shaping a karmically balanced life.

By recognizing the interconnectedness of all living things and embracing sustainable practices, individuals can contribute positively to the environment and foster harmony within the broader tapestry of existence. Ultimately, "Living the Karma Way" is an invitation to embark on a journey of self-discovery, conscious living, and the cultivation of positive karma for a fulfilling and harmonious life.

In recapitulating the key concepts of "Living the Karma Way" it becomes evident that this book serves as a comprehensive manual for those seeking a transformative and purposeful life. Beginning with a thorough exploration of karma's historical and cultural context, this book lays a foundation for understanding the intricate threads of cause and effect that shape our existence.

The purpose of the guide becomes clear—to empower individuals with practical wisdom to navigate life's complexities and cultivate positive habits. From unraveling the three types of karma to emphasizing the interconnectedness of actions, this book encourages readers to explore the ripple effect of their choices. Practical applications, such as mindfulness practices and meditation techniques, are presented to foster a conscious and intentional way of living.

The book concludes by highlighting the importance of compassion, empathy, and ethical decision-making in contributing to a karmically balanced life. In essence, "Living the Karma Way" encapsulates a holistic approach to personal growth, environmental responsibility, and harmonious living, inviting readers on a journey toward a more fulfilling and purpose-driven existence. Encouragement for continuous growth serves as a guiding light for individuals committed to the ongoing journey of self-improvement and personal evolution.

Rooted in the belief that growth is a lifelong process, this book provides invaluable insights and practical encouragement for navigating the challenges and triumphs inherent in the pursuit of continuous development. Through the exploration of key concepts such as resilience, mindfulness, and the power of positive intention, readers are equipped with tools to foster personal and professional growth.

The emphasis on embracing change, learning from mistakes, and cultivating a growth mindset underscores the transformative potential of challenges. By encouraging readers to view setbacks as opportunities, this book inspires a resilient and optimistic approach to life's ever-evolving landscape. Ultimately, encouragement for continuous growth is a testament to the enduring human spirit, urging individuals to embrace the journey of growth with courage, curiosity, and a steadfast commitment to becoming the best versions of themselves.

The transformative power of living a karma-centered life is profound and far-reaching. By embracing the principles of cause and effect, individuals embark on a journey of self-discovery and conscious living. The awareness that every thought, intention, and action contribute to the intricate web of karma empowers individuals to shape their destinies with purpose and mindfulness. This transformative journey involves unraveling negative patterns, cultivating positive habits, and recognizing the interconnectedness of all living things.

The practice of mindfulness, ethical decision-making, and compassion becomes a compass for navigating life's challenges. Living a karma-centered life fosters personal growth, resilience, and a deep sense of responsibility for one's impact on the world. It is an invitation to create a harmonious existence by aligning actions with positive intentions, contributing positively to the collective tapestry of cause and effect that weaves through every aspect of life. In essence, the transformative power lies in the conscious choice to cultivate positive karma, influencing not only individual well-being but also fostering a more harmonious and interconnected world.

Inspirational Message from The Bodhisattva

"Living the Karma Way " beckons us to embark on a transformative journey, weaving the ancient wisdom of karma philosophy into the fabric of our modern lives. This guide is not just a book; it is an invitation to embrace a life rich in purpose and conscious choices. It reminds us that each thought, action, and intention ripples through the intricate tapestry of existence, shaping our destiny and influencing the world around us. As we explore the practical applications offered, from unraveling negative patterns to cultivating mindful awareness, we discover the power to sculpt our lives into a masterpiece of fulfillment and balance. This guide inspires us to navigate the complexities of our journey with grace, resilience, and compassion, recognizing the interconnectedness of all living things. In the embrace of karma's guiding light, let us find the courage to live authentically, make ethical choices, and contribute positively to the collective symphony of life. "Living the Karma Way" is more than a guide, it is a beacon illuminating the path to a life that resonates with purpose, harmony, and the boundless possibilities of positive transformation. This is the way... Namaste...

Appendices and Resources

The appendices for "Living the Karma Way" serve as valuable supplementary resources, enhancing the reader's understanding and practical application of the book's teachings. These appendices may include additional exercises, meditation techniques, and reflective prompts designed to deepen the reader's engagement with key concepts.

Reference materials, glossaries, and further readings might be provided to support comprehensive comprehension. Inclusion of real-life case studies or stories could illustrate the practical implications of karma-centered living.

Additionally, the appendices may offer practical guides for incorporating mindfulness practices into daily routines or implementing positive habits. Overall, the appendices serve as a toolkit, equipping readers with practical tools and resources to enrich their journey towards a more fulfilling and harmonious life based on the principles outlined in the main text.

Guided Meditation Scripts

Guided Meditation for Inner Peace and Relaxation

Begin by finding a comfortable seated position, either on a chair or cushion. Close your eyes gently and take a few deep breaths, allowing your body to relax with each exhale.

Now, shift your attention to your breath. Feel the natural flow of your breath as you inhale and exhale. Notice the sensation of the breath entering and leaving your body.

As you breathe, imagine a soft, warm light surrounding you. This light represents calm and peace. With each breath, allow this light to expand, filling your entire body with a soothing energy.

Bring your awareness to any areas of tension or discomfort in your body. As you exhale, visualize releasing this tension, letting it dissolve into the air. Feel your muscles becoming loose and relaxed.

Now, let your mind's eye take you to a tranquil place in nature. It could be a peaceful beach, a serene forest, or a quiet meadow. Imagine the sights, sounds, and scents of this place. Feel a deep sense of peace and connection with the natural world.

As you continue to breathe, envision any thoughts or worries as clouds passing by in the sky. Acknowledge them without judgment and allow them to drift away, leaving your mind clear and calm.

Bring your attention back to the present moment. Feel the gentle rise and fall of your chest with each breath. Sense the stillness within and around you.

Take a moment to express gratitude for this time of relaxation and self-care. When you're ready, slowly open your eyes, bringing the sense of tranquility with you into the rest of your day.

Worksheets for Self-Reflection

Feel free to customize these worksheets based on your preferences or specific areas of focus. Self-reflection is a personal journey, so encourage individuals to tailor these worksheets to meet their unique needs and goals.

Daily, Weekly, or Monthly Reflections Journal

Date:

What were the three most significant events or moments of today?

How did I feel during those moments?

What did I learn about myself today?

Is there anything I would like to improve or change?

Goal Setting and Progress:

Goal:

Specific steps I can take to achieve this goal:

Progress made so far:

Obstacles encountered:

Adjustments or changes needed:

Strengths and Areas for Growth:

List three personal strengths:

1.)

2.)

3.)

List three areas for growth:

1.)

2.)

3.)

How can I leverage my strengths to address areas for growth?

Values Alignment:

List five values that are important to me (e.g., honesty, compassion, creativity):

1.)

2.)

3.)

4.)
5.)
Reflect on recent decisions or actions. Did they align with these values?
Mindfulness and Well-being:
Daily mindfulness practice (e.g., meditation, deep breathing):
How did I prioritize self-care today?
One thing that brought me joy today:
What thoughts or feelings do I need to acknowledge and release?
Gratitude Journal:
List three things I am grateful for today:
1.)
2.)
3.)
How did expressing gratitude make me feel?

Recommended Reading List

These books offer diverse perspectives, and it's beneficial to explore various sources to deepen your understanding of the karma way of life. Additionally, personal experiences and reflections play a significant role in embodying these principles in your daily existence.

"The Bhagavad Gita" by Eknath Easwaran *An ancient Indian scripture that explores the concept of dharma (righteous duty) and the path of selfless action.*

"The Art of Happiness" by Dalai Lama and Howard Cutler *A guide that combines the wisdom of the Dalai Lama with Western psychology, offering insights into the pursuit of happiness.*

"The Power of Now" by Eckhart Tolle *Tolle explores the concept of living in the present moment and the transformative power of mindfulness.*

"Radical Acceptance" by Tara Brach *Tara Brach combines mindfulness and self-compassion to guide readers toward accepting themselves and their lives.*

"The Four Agreements" by Don Miguel Ruiz *Offers a code of conduct based on ancient Toltec wisdom, providing practical principles for personal freedom and fulfillment.*

"The Miracle of Mindfulness" by Thich Nhat Hanh *Thich Nhat Hanh introduces mindfulness practices, emphasizing the importance of being fully present in each moment.*

"The Karma of Brown Folk" by Vijay Prashad *Explores the concept of karma in the context of South Asian history, politics, and diaspora.*

"The Seven Spiritual Laws of Success" by Deepak Chopra *Deepak Chopra outlines spiritual principles that can lead to success and fulfillment in various aspects of life.*

"The Untethered Soul" by Michael A. Singer *Explores the concept of self and consciousness, offering insights on letting go of limitations and experiencing inner freedom.*

"The Tibetan Book of Living and Dying" by Sogyal Rinpoche *A guide to life and death from a Tibetan Buddhist perspective, offering wisdom on living with purpose and preparing for death.*

Recommended Websites:

Explore these websites with an open mind, as they offer diverse perspectives on living a mindful and purposeful life in alignment with karma philosophy.

Chopra Center: *Chopra Center[1]: Founded by Deepak Chopra, this center provides resources on mindfulness, meditation, and holistic well-being.*

Mindful.org: Mindful[2]: *Offers articles, guided meditations, and resources to support a mindful and balanced lifestyle.*

Lions Roar: Lions Roar[3]: *A source for Buddhist teachings, including articles on karma, meditation, and mindfulness.*

Tricycle: The Buddhist Review: *Tricycle[4]: A Buddhist publication covering a wide range of topics related to Buddhist philosophy and practices.*

Yoga Journal: Yoga [5]Journal: *Provides information on yoga, meditation, and holistic living.*

BuddhaNet: BuddhaNet[6]: *An online Buddhist education and information network with resources on meditation and teachings.*

Dharma Seed: *Offers a vast collection of audio teachings from various meditation teachers, allowing you to explore different perspectives on mindfulness.*

Buddhist Door: *Covers a wide range of topics related to Buddhism, including teachings on karma and mindful living.*

Spirituality & Practice: *Provides resources on spiritual wisdom from various traditions, including articles on karma and mindful living.*

---

1. https://chopra.com/

2. https://www.mindful.org/

3. https://www.lionsroar.com/

4. https://tricycle.org/

5. https://app.designrr.io/

6. https://www.buddhanet.net/

Don't miss out!

Visit the website below and you can sign up to receive emails whenever Randy Woodrum publishes a new book. There's no charge and no obligation.

https://books2read.com/r/B-A-TKUCB-EXUTC

BOOKS 2 READ

Connecting independent readers to independent writers.